NEW ORLEANS JAZZ STYLES

CW00411299

FOREWORD

One of the really significant contributions of the Twentieth Century to music ... and a strictly American development ...is the jazz idiom. Although authorities are not in complete agreement, many believe that this spontaneous movement had its origin in New Orleans, in the honky-tonk amusement section of the city, centered around Basin Street. From there, it spread northward up the Mississippi Valley to Memphis, St. Louis, Kansas City, Chicago, and eastward to New York. During the past century American jazz in its popular forms has captured the imagination of musicians throughout the world, and it has enriched with new rhythms and harmonies much of the serious music of our time.

While the development of its counterpart in New York and other more cosmopolitan centres of the U.S.A. has attained much sophistication and refinement, New Orleans jazz has remained simple and close to the source of its origin. In this collection it is the intention of the composer to present basic examples ranging from a genuine blues treatment in "Mississippi Mud", through a relaxed and humourous "Dixieland Combo" in the spirit of the early 1920's, to an intensely rhythmic, brassy and defiant arrangement of the "Frankie and Johnny" folk ballad.

NEW ORLEANS JAZZ STYLES offers the average piano player new opportunities to experience the New Orleans style. I would like to encourage you to deviate from the written notes with your own improvisations if so desired, for spontaneity is an essential ingredient of jazz.

WILLIAM GILLOCK

NEW ORLEANS JAZZ STYLES

First published 1992
The Willis Music Co.

Exclusive distributors:
Music Sales Limited, 8/9 Frith Street, London W1V 5TZ.
Music Sales Pty Limited, 120 Rothschild Avenue, Rosebery, NSW 2018, Australia

Reproducing this music in any form is illegal and forbidden
by the Copyright, Designs and Patents Act 1988.

NEW ORLEANS NIGHTFALL

SONG STYLE; SOMEWHAT FLEXIBLY (♩ = about 54)

WILLIAM GILLOCK

FASTER, with a beat (♩ = about 160)

© MCMLXV, by The Willis Music Co.
International Copyright Secured

THE CONSTANT BASS

WILLIAM GILLOCK

light staccato throughout

© MCMLXV, by The Willis Music Co.
International Copyright Secured

MARDI GRAS

WILLIAM GILLOCK

© MCMLXV, by The Willis Music Co.
International Copyright Secured

DIXIELAND COMBO

WILLIAM GILLOCK

UNSOPHISTICATED; in the early jazz style ($\bullet$ = about 152)

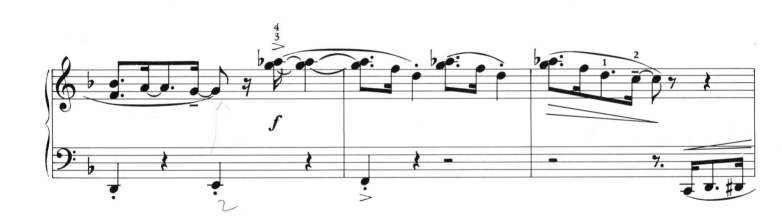

© MCMLXV, by The Willis Music Co.
International Copyright Secured

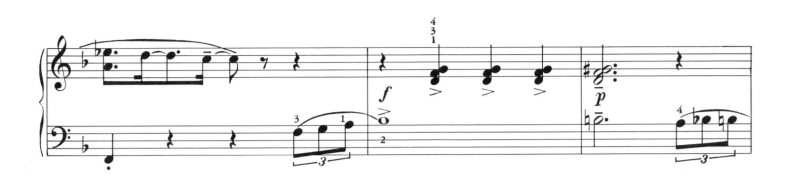

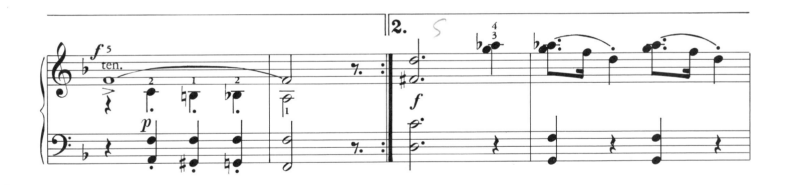

FRANKIE AND JOHNNY
(THEME AND VARIATIONS)

WILLIAM GILLOCK

Bold and Brassy (♩ = about 176)

THEME

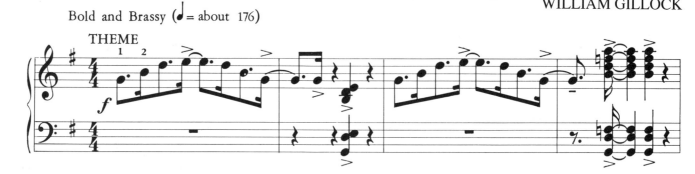

VAR. I

© MCMLXV, by The Willis Music Co.
International Copyright Secured

NEW ORLEANS BLUES

Slow blues tempo ♩ = about 80

WILLIAM GILLOCK

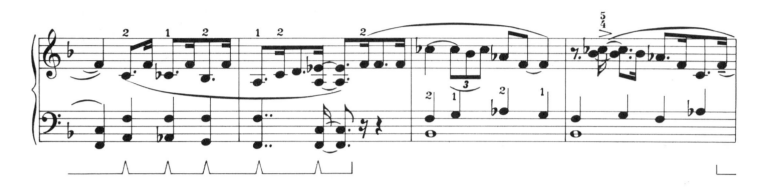

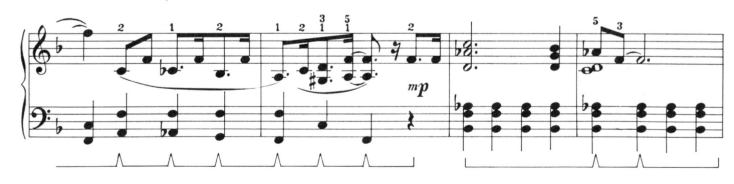

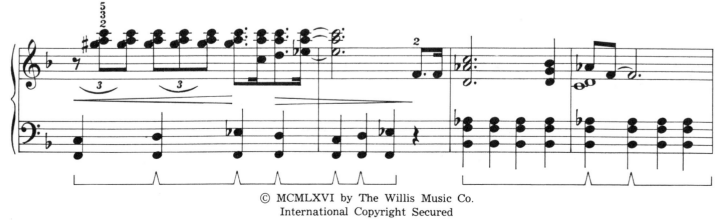

© MCMLXVI by The Willis Music Co.
International Copyright Secured

TAKING IT EASY

WILLIAM GILLOCK

AFTER MIDNIGHT

With reserve and sophistication ♩ = 144 - 168

WILLIAM GILLOCK

MISTER TRUMPET MAN

With a pronounced beat ♩= 100 – 116

WILLIAM GILLOCK

BOURBON STREET SATURDAY NIGHT

Loud and Brassy ♩ = 132–144

WILLIAM GILLOCK

MISSISSIPPI MUD

WILLIAM GILLOCK

With a lazy beat (♩ = 92)

© MCMLXXVII by The Willis Music Co.
International Copyright Secured

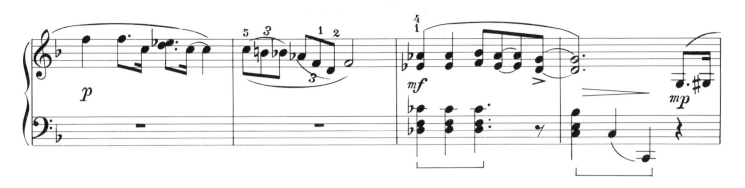

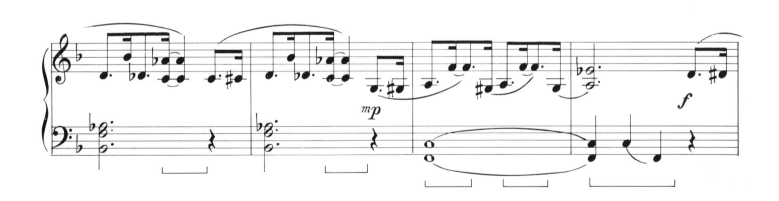

UPTOWN BLUES

WILLIAM GILLOCK

DOWNTOWN BEAT

WILLIAM GILLOCK

CANAL STREET BLUES

WILLIAM GILLOCK

BILL BAILEY

WON'T YOU PLEASE COME HOME

HUGHIE CANON
Arr. WILLIAM GILLOCK

light staccato throughout, like a plucked string bass

Printed in Great Britain by Commercial Colour Press, 2/96 (23502).